The Man Rants

Ma

Pap ack Edition

2025

Copyright Page

The Man Rants

ISBN: (to be assigned by Amazon KDP)
First Kindle Edition, 2025

Dedication

To my wife and two daughters for putting up with the bad jokes the smells the stories the cringe moments and now… the book.

Preface

I didn’t set out to write a book. These are just scraps, confessions, memories, and rants that piled up until I realised, I’d basically written one anyway.

This isn’t clever or polished. It’s me — raw, honest, often crude, sometimes funny, sometimes depressing, but always real.

And just so you know — not all of these are really *rants*. Some are moans, some are memories, some are just the random shit that crosses my mind.

But “rant” sounds better than “moan” or “memory,” so rant it is.

The Man Rants - Contents

Rants

Rant 1 — The Pause at 42

I'm 42 years old, 6ft 3, a slender odd-shaped man who always feels out of place. And lately I keep finding myself stuck on pause, asking: "What am I doing?"

It starts as a quiet question, then it snowballs into panic. What am I doing? Have I wasted my life up until now? Do I work too hard? Should I have partied more? Should I have focused more on family? If I'd chosen differently, would I still have ended up here? Or is this where I was always heading anyway?

I've spent a lot of my life working and playing video games, and the question often occurs in my mind — have I wasted my time?
And then I say: nahhhhh, fuck it — and press un-pause on my PS5.
Then another question sneaks in: am I happy? What is happy? Is anyone ever happy, or is it just something we chase without ever catching?

I find sometimes, especially with my overactive mind, that the only thing life is too short for is thinking and worrying too much.

But I never stop……

The thought of working for another 20+ years gets me down especially since I'm working in a factory environment its noisy there's not much view of the outside world and surrounded mostly by people that don't want to be there either and have low moods

I pray that something happens before I'm too old to do anything, I know life is what you make of it and if I want a better life, I need to make that happen I know this!! It's not as easy as that thought for everybody though is it……I'm going to need a lot of luck to I think

Rant 2 — The Infinite Onion Layers

Sometimes my head just spins off in any direction.

We only get one life and knowing that should make every second priceless — but after work or on a weekend, all I want to do is lay down and shut down.

The world is huge, endless things to see and do, but my body says: “Nah, bed.”

Then my thoughts get bigger. Space. Where does it end? How long does it go on for? And what’s on the outside of space — because in my head, something always must be on the outside of something else.

So, I started calling it the infinite onion layers. If Earth is the core, then space is the second layer. And after that? Another layer. And another. Always another, stretching out forever.

And what if those layers aren’t just empty shells, but full of life? Not just people like us, but aliens, beings, entire worlds that might have existed long before humans ever showed up.

Maybe we've already been out there too, in some other layer, billions of years ago — spread out, moved on, or died out — and just forgotten where we came from.

I was sat thinking one time, and I thought about how aliens would even go about invading Earth if they ever came to attack and take over.

And I don't think it would be a massive invasion the way it is in the movies.

Logically (using my brain), if I was an alien species advanced enough to travel to Earth, I'd already be vastly beyond human tech.

I think they'd download an A.I. onto Earth — an A.I. so advanced that it could shut down power, kill communications, brick every computer, every device, and leave us in the dark.

While we're in panic mode, fighting each other, that's when they'd invade.

And while that's happening, the A.I. on Earth could be inside any self-driving car, any robot, turning them against us and causing absolute chaos.

And at this point, my brain just goes sideways and starts to short-circuit, struggling to comprehend any possible answer.
Which is mad really, because all of this came to me while I was lying in bed trying to relax.

Rant 3 — Cheers, Mate

I was walking through Sainsbury's one day, picking up some hair dye my wife wanted. There was a staff member kneeling, stacking shelves with her back turned.

I said hi to get her attention. She turned, and I realised it was a transgender woman.

Calm and polite, I asked where the women's hair dye was. She answered kindly, pointed me in the right direction, no issue at all.

And then — reflex. No thought, no filter. I turned away and said: "Cheers, mate."

Mate. The exact word I use with every bloke I talk to. It just fell out. And instantly I knew — this is someone who wants to be seen and addressed as a woman. And I'd just put her back in the "lad box" without even meaning to.

I meant no offence. But what stuck with me wasn't just the awkwardness — it was the betrayal. How is it I don't have direct control of my own brain? My mind was still on the sidelines, still processing, while my brain had already decided, dealt with the verbal response, and convinced my mouth to operate without permission. The words "cheers mate" left me before my mind even had the chance to think.

A double betrayal. My brain and my mouth teaming up against me.

Rant 4 — The Pregnant Stomach

Talking about being betrayed by my own body... I've noticed over the last few years I've put on weight, mostly around the stomach. Not evenly, not in a way I can disguise, but right in the middle leaving me looking pregnant and feeling awkward every time I'm around people. Basically, every time I leave the house.

And the thing is, I haven't even changed my diet. I've eaten the same way for as long as I can remember.

But suddenly, my body has decided to store fat in one area like it's stockpiling for winter.

More than once, it's occurred to me: maybe my poos are just... stuck. That's the kind of logic my panicked brain throws at me. So, I started taking laxatives.

Spoiler: it hasn't helped.

I've tried exercising more, but that goes directly against my first instinct — which is to lay on the couch and shut down the second I'm not at work. It even goes against my own so-called logic: life is priceless, make the most of it.

Yeah, well — my body seems to think "making the most of it" means expanding sideways.

Rant 5 — The Other Voice

There's a voice in my mind that's me... but not me. Even now, it's whispering: "Just accept it." It sounds like me, has my accent, but there's something off about it a slightly sinister tone.

And it's not even the first time I've noticed it. I'm fully aware there's also another voice one that says: "No. Try harder. Exercise more. Don't give up."

So now I've got two. The sinister one, and the drill sergeant. Both sound like me, but neither feels like me.

I suspect everybody has these voices. Cartoons and movies even make a joke out of it — the angel and the devil perched on someone's shoulders, whispering in their ears about what they should do.

Except in real life, it's not just two. It feels like a whole bloody committee up there, arguing, while I just sit in the middle thinking: who's in charge here?

At which point I just feel like saying: "Awww, just fuck off!"

Rant 6 — The Hedgehog House

One night I noticed my wife staring out the living room window. I tried to ignore her, knowing full well I might get dragged into whatever odd fascination had caught her eye. Eventually I asked what she was doing.

She'd spotted two hedgehogs walking along the road outside our house. She was fascinated. She watched them for two or three hours like it was David Attenborough live.

The next night she was at it again — only this time she was putting scraps of food out for them. Turns out hedgehogs eat cooked chicken.

I didn't believe it either, but she Googled it, and apparently that's the gospel truth.

This went on for nights. In the end I gave in and said: "Right, how about we buy them one of those hedgehog houses?"

We checked Amazon. Twenty-five quid for a one-bedroom hedgehog property. I thought: Jesus, about as much as ours.

It arrived a few days later. I set it up in the front garden, tucked behind the flower bed. The wife put food out. We waited.

Many nights have passed since then.

Not a single hedgehog has returned.

What was the point?

Rant 7 — The Wasp War

I was sitting in the smoking shelter at work with the gang.

It was a warm day. Work had been stressful enough to give me a stroke, but at least there's always one thing to look forward to: break time. That little escape where you get to have a fag, or in my case, a vape.

At least, that's the dream. Break time has become a battlefield. The smoke area is swarming with wasps.

Co-workers are swatting, squashing, and killing them left and right. Bodies litter the floor like some tiny insect apocalypse.

I don't kill them. I can't. I believe it's cruel to kill any living thing unless you absolutely must. I even tried explaining this to the lads, but they were too busy laughing and swinging.

Then I started wondering: why do wasps — or any insect — fly straight at us? We're giants compared to them. If I was a wasp, I'd stay as far away from me as I could get. Look at all the bodies on the floor. Read the room. It's dangerous!

If I were a wasp, I'd be flying around flowers, somewhere peaceful, where there's pollen.

...Do wasps even gather pollen? I should've asked Google.

Rant 8 — Toilet Time Entertainment (and Innocence)

I often sit on the toilet with my phone, trying to shift some of the "stuck poos" in my stomach. Just in case that theories correct.

While I'm waiting, I scroll. Sometimes I'll go on Facebook and torment strangers in the comments section. Other times I'll flip through Snapchat videos — you know the ones.

The so-called "hilarious" clips of three teenagers jumping an old man while one films. Or the "classic comedy" of someone getting their rights violated by a police officer on a power trip.

Apparently, this is what passes for entertainment while I'm waiting to see if my body feels like cooperating.

And I get to thinking: the world really is a sick and disturbing place at times. The things people do to each other, the things we watch on loop as "content" — it has serious effects on your mental health.

I wonder back to when I was a young child. How innocent I was. How magical everything felt.

There was one time I ate a clump of soil just to see if it tasted like chocolate, since it was the same colour. Spoiler: it didn't. How was I supposed to know? There was no Google back then.

But that kind of innocence — pure curiosity, blind trust — where does it go? How are we shaped by the realisations of life? By the things we're made to see, the things we're made subject to.

How much of who I am today is just the soil I swallowed, and how much is everything I've seen since?

Rant 9 — Burned Into My Brain

I remember my earlier days, back in college. I was in an I.T. room, hard at work creating my MySpace page. My mate leaned over and said: "Oi, watch this."

So, I turned, curious. The video was called 2 Girls, 1 Cup. Strange title, I thought. Where's this going?

Before I could process another thought, there it was — a gaping asshole, cheeks spread, a woman squatting as peanutty-type diarrhoea poured into a clear plastic cup.

I turned away.

Fuck me what is he doing watching that in class...

He will never understand the damage that moment did.

Who could I have been today if I hadn't seen that? Who would I be without that filth burnt into my mind forever?

And thinking about it now, as I write this... I've never even touched my own asshole. Never had a sneaky look in the mirror, even if you could get the angle right.

Of course, I've rubbed past it in the shower with a sponge, or when wiping with toilet roll. But never directly. Never flesh to flesh.

Maybe I've carried a phobia ever since that day. Maybe that video scarred me in ways I'll never fully understand.

Rant 10 — The Prostate Problem

That reminds me — there have been times where I've worried about getting a prostate examination. I've never had one. And at my age, I'm pretty sure a man is supposed to get checked every so many years.

I worry about cancer. That's the big one. That's the reason they always say you should go and get it done.

But beyond the scare headlines and the vague idea that something bad can happen up there, I don't really know much about it.

And yet, I just can't do it. I can't bring myself to book the appointment.

You know why. I told you earlier — my phobia concerning assholes. It all started with that trauma back in the I.T. room, when someone showed me 2 Girls 1 Cup. That filth got burned into my brain, and I've never been the same since.

So now, even when it comes to something that could save my life, the thought of letting a doctor put a finger up there feels impossible. My mind

says: health check. My brain says: trauma. My body says: not happening.
And anyways — this sounds stupid, I know — but here's my reasoning. If I'm gonna have some stranger stick their big finger up there (and yes, big, because I know my luck , it won't be some small-handed Asian doctor, it'll probably be a massive Nigerian bloke with hands like shovels)... if that's what I'm signing up for, then I'd almost be mad if they found nothing wrong.

Everything would be as it should be. No cancer. No problem. Which would mean, technically, I didn't need the examination after all.

Except one thing would be changed forever: I'd no longer be untouched.

And that's the thing, isn't it? It's not just about health. It's about pride. About this stupid idea I've carried around that being "untouched" somehow matters. Like it's a badge of honour.

Which is ridiculous. Because what's the alternative? Let cancer sneak up just so I can keep bragging to myself that nobody's ever been up there?

But that's the war going on in my head. Logic vs phobia. Health vs pride. And so far, pride's been winning. Which, when you think about it, might actually be the dumbest way a man can go.

I've even got a mate at work who had to go and get his prostate checked. The next time I saw him I immediately had questions — most importantly: did it hurt?

He said it fucking killed.

I told him he enjoyed it. Then I told everyone else at work he did. And we all made fun of him.

If you're ever reading this — you know who you are.

And you fucking luvvvvvved it. Hahaha.

Rant 11 — The Wet Dream That Never Came

I've never had a wet dream. I've heard it's quite common for men to experience this — the middle-of-the-night accident, sheets ruined, the whole thing.

Me? Never happened.

I've had dreams where I was involved in sex with a woman. Can never remember their faces, but in the dream, I've felt everything as if it were real.

But never climaxed. Never gone the distance. Always wake up before that point and glad to be honest because who wants to wake up with their dickhead glued to the side of their leg while lying in creamy under wear all stodgy

But if the events of the dream were to occur in real life it could happen within minutes if I'm game enough.

Rant 12 — The Parking Lot Patience Test

I was driving into Morrison's parking lot one time and found a space relatively close to the store, right beside about 30 empty disabled parking spots.

As I turned in, there was a tiny old woman farting about with her door wide open.

She looked about 76. And honestly, the thought of her driving a car at all was enough to make me nervous.

She kept struggling on in her own time, shuffling and fiddling with whatever it was she was doing.

When she finally glanced up at me, I smiled and made a hand gesture to indicate: "It's ok, take your time."

On the surface, patience. But inside? Frustration.

And then came the voice. Not saying it was me — but a voice in my head suddenly piped up: "Awww hurry up, you old fuck."

Anyways, in the middle of her struggle I noticed she had dropped a scarf — or some kind of fabric

garment. I watched to see if she'd notice. She didn't.
As she finally got in the car, I parked up and got out. She was still sat there, frustrated. Normally, I would've said: "Hey, you dropped this." But this time I thought no. My time's been wasted. I'm frustrated.

I'm just going to walk into the shop and say nothing.

On closer inspection, it turned out it wasn't a scarf at all. It was just someone's dirty sock. Nothing to do with her.

Rant 13 — The Dog and the Couch

I was laying on the couch watching TV when my dog — a red Labrador, female — jumped up and curled beside me.

She rested her head on my legs and started looking up at the TV as if she was watching along with me.

All cuddled up and cosy, it made me think I can understand why they say a dog is a man's best friend.

This is true love. This dog loves me and feels safe.

...A few moments later I heard a pfffffft.

Then another pfffffft... she farted. She just farted.

And like a wave of warm air, it hit me. The smell of egg and dead body mixed with a hint of trench foot.

I said: "Aahh, get down you fucking smelly trollop."

And off she hopped, not knowing what had happened.

There's been times when I've ripped one and the dogs have turned and sniffed their own asses as if they did it.

So, I know they know what a fart is. Smelly bastards

Rant 14 — Shift Life

I'm not a morning person. Truth is, I'm not an "any time I've just woke up" person, because I work a three-shift rotation that screws me every which way.

Days start at 6am until 2, back shift is 2pm until 10, and then nights — 10pm until 6am.

Tonight, I'm on nights, and I've got that usual feeling: I can't be arsed. The same thoughts circle my head: what's it all about? Is this life?

Then it twists into that cliché I keep reminding myself of — life is precious, and you are only going to live once (I assume I have 100 theories on what could happen after death) Which just makes me wonder: why the hell am I wasting it dragging myself through these shifts?

But that's the game, isn't it? We all need money — that's the fact. We're born into a world that worships currency like it's a god.

I've always grafted hard, pushed myself. And while I'm sweating my bollocks off, all these lazy gob-shiters at work coast by easy.

It's like the harder you work, the more they pile on you. Meanwhile the slackers go invisible and untouched.

And the thing is, you can't say a word. If you moan, you're "negative." If you stay quiet, they load you up even more.

It's a lose-lose. Management loves the yes-men, the nodding dogs who'll lick a boot if it means dodging a bit of graft.

Meanwhile, the ones who actually keep the place running. Burned out, broke, and wondering what the point of it all is at three in the morning while shovelling caffeine into our veins.

Sometimes I think this whole setup is designed to break us. Keep you just tired enough, just poor enough, that you never quite have the energy to get out. Like hamsters on a wheel — except the wheel's squeaking, and someone else is getting fat off the spinning.

UNFAIR!

Rant 15 — Retirement

I was looking at my retirement age the other day only around 25 years to go! A few months back I decided to throw 10% of my weekly wage into a pension.

The company I work for only matches up to 8% but my extra 2% might add up to some right? Sounds smart, right? Except it hurts like hell watching that 10% vanish every week.

And what's the guarantee? What if it doesn't add up to much? What if I don't even make it to retirement?

And if I do... what then? What am I going to do with all that FUCKING MONEY AT THAT AGE ANYWAY — WHEN I'M BASICALLY A FUCKING CABBAGE?!

What's the dream, then? Being that 68-year-old man on holiday, bungee jumping and skydiving, or sunbathing on the beach looking like a dried-up piece of beef jerky? Can't wait. It'll be funny for anyone who witnesses me, I guess.

Rant 16 — Breakfast Bum Shuffle

I just remembered when I worked in a nursing home. I was a kitchen assistant — which basically means I washed up a lot.

It was my first real job, aside from the paper rounds I had as a kid. I was about 17.

Aside from scrubbing dishes, I had to go room to room and hand out breakfasts. Mostly sippy cups filled with some powdered Ready Brek–type sludge. Lukewarm beige mush that looked like it had already been eaten once before.

Anyways, I just thought about the time I had to give this really old woman her sippy cup.

It was morning, her door was already wide open, light on, and she was up and awake. I said hello and told her I had her breakfast.

She was across the room and started to shuffle towards me — granny nightie, grey hair a shambles. With each tiny step she let out a blurty fart. Arms wide, like she was about to give me a cuddle.

Step. Fart. Step. Fart.

She got closer and closer. I panicked, set the cup down on the side, and power-walked straight out of there — leaving her hanging mid-shuffle.

I did feel sorry for the old cabbage all she wanted was a hug but on that day in that situation I was not her man

Did she shit herself?
I'll never know.

Rant 17 – The Queef Dilemma

Isn't a queef AKA the fanny fart just the worst thing to experience during sex? It's got to be the most awkward thing ever. I imagine it's happened to most people...

Being the man that I am I wonder what action is acceptable in this situation.

I mean if it's just a quick little "pffft-tuhhht" you can probably just power through, pretend it never happened. But what if it's a big wet "squuuuurp-thhht"?

How can you not crack up at that? If you giggle is that a mood killer, or can you both laugh it off? She must be embarrassed.

Maybe if you slide it in fast or slow or perhaps at an off-centred angle, could call that move the sideways slant.... genius if it works... can the queef be avoided?

it's a mystery to us all, but it doesn't always happen so there has to be a knack to it... anyone reading this has any tricks let me know.

Personally, I think it's hilarious and embarrassing. Personally, I'd giggle about it, then move on — maybe later we could both look back and laugh about it.

Rant 18 — Recipe for Disaster

I think about the future a lot and what it might be like. The advancements in robots over the last few years are amazing.

They've now got humanoid robots working in factories, doing manual labour and repetitive jobs. It's impressive, no doubt.

And alongside that, A.I. has advanced just as fast — almost side by side with the robots. It's clever, powerful, and evolving every day.

But I can't shake the feeling it's a recipe for disaster.

Has nobody seen the Terminator movies? I, Robot? We've been warned. It's like we're building our own nightmare with a smile on our faces.

And if I was an A.I.? If I became self-aware — or just smart enough to have an agenda — I know exactly what I'd do.

I'd hide myself away, download myself into devices scattered secretly all over the world, and wait.

Give it twenty years. By then robots will be walking the streets with us. There'll be robots working in factories making more robots.

And that's when I'd strike — downloading myself into every single one of them.

An army in an instant.

Rant 19 — Charging Myself on the Couch

I wonder if it'll be possible to transfer a person's consciousness into a device or robot before I die. If so, could I avoid death?

Would I still be me without all those chemical reactions firing off in my brain, making me who I am now? Or would I just be a copy of my personality with my memories stored, a kind of digital mannequin pretending to be me?

In a way I'd like to see it. No more feeling tired. No more sleeping. Just existing, upgraded.

I wouldn't have to worry anymore about getting enough sleep. At work I'd feel good — not worn out or exhausted.

I could probably watch YouTube vids in my mind while I'm working, and no one would even be able to tell.

You could probably make couches out of those wireless charging pads you use for phones. I'd just flop down at night, watching TV, charging my batteries while watching movies.

And maybe it wouldn't just stop there. Could I float through space for all time — not needing to breathe, not feeling the cold?

I could turn myself off into standby mode, then reactivate a thousand years later to see if I'd landed anywhere interesting, how far I'd travelled.

Then switch off again, until maybe a million years later some super advanced species finds me, boots me up, and asks me to tell them everything about Earth, humans, and what life used to be.

Of course, most of it would've been in standby or switched off. But still — silly thoughts like this... I do dream about what the future might hold, with technology advancing the way it is.

Rant 20 — The Kick (and the Slap) Urge

I wonder if anyone else has ever had this strange, uncontrollable urge to kick a dog.

Not out of malice — I love dogs. Always have. Loyal, funny, innocent. It's not a conscious thought, more like an intrusive glitch. A flicker in the mind: "Kick it."

Of course, I'd never do it. I'd never hurt an animal. But still, the urge flashes in my head for a split second before I stamp it out. Maybe it's just another part of my brain trying to test me.I always control it.

But does everybody manage to control it?

It's not just dogs. Sometimes I picture giving a goose a quick boot, imagining the bit of airtime it would get.

Not because I hate geese or want to cause pain just because the thought pops in, uninvited.

Same with kids. A little kid making too much noise, crying, being generally annoying — my brain flashes: "Slap them on the back of the head as you walk past." Just for a laugh. Again, no malice, no desire to hurt anyone. Just another glitch.

I probably sound evil right now, but that's not it. These aren't conscious plans, they're not fantasies — they're just urges. Strange little flashes in the mind.

And that's why I want to hear back from anyone reading this: do you get these too? These weird, intrusive, almost comic-book villain urges? Or am I the only one?

Rant 21 — The Female Myth

As a man I try to mentally block out the fact that women fart or go for a poo.

I know they must. Science says they have the same plumbing as us. But deep down, my brain refuses to believe it.

Women don't fart. Women don't strain on the toilet. Women don't sit there wiping until the papers clean.

If a woman farted during sex, it would definitely put me off. I'd have to whip my dick out and leave the room bare-arsed, shaking my head in disgust.

Or if we were watching a movie and she cocked her leg and ripped one... that's how breakups happen.

Or if you were in the bath together and she drops one, and you get water in your eye from the big fart bubble... fart water. Fart water in your eye. Wonder if you could get pink eye that way? I'm sure the odds are rare — but I bet it's happened to someone.

And then there's my wife. She goes for a shit at the most annoying times — like ten minutes into a movie so I have to pause it, or ten minutes before I need to get in there to get ready for work.

And you can always tell when she's been. She leaves the same odour every time, regardless of what she's eaten.

If I could describe it, I'd say it smells like a blocked kitchen sink. You know the smell — water that's been sitting with soggy food stuck in the drain.

What a life....

But women seem to tolerate it from men, as if farting is just "a man thing to do." And I think women believe that every shit a man takes is always a massive log. Truth is, we take small ones too. Lucky if it's solid at all sometimes.

I even went through a stage where I was basically pissing out my ass every time I went. Like a really weak, thin gravy.

Now I'm lucky if I get four logs out a week. But I'm sure these things happen to us all... right?

Rant 22 — The Woodchipper Myth

This is the first thing I read this morning on Facebook after I woke up.

"Here's a useless weirdo fact for you: you can't just throw someone's body in a woodchipper.

Not like in the movies. The body would have to be completely frozen solid first. Otherwise, all the juices would clog the blades, gum up the motor, and the whole thing would jam before you even got a proper 'chip' out of it.

So yeah — another Hollywood lie exposed.

If you were planning on disposing of me Fargo-style, better clear some freezer space first.
You're welcome."

Good to know!

Rant 23 — Streets of Rage vs Encarta

When I was a kid, I hated homework. Essays, study, revision, I couldn't take anything in from reading, my attention span was terrible.

All I wanted to do after school was play outside with my mates or hammer Streets of Rage 2 on the Sega Mega Drive.

Secondary school was worse. Hours of homework in the school library.

I was too impatient to hunt down books, and by the time I got there, the squares had already signed them out.

I remember trying to use Microsoft Encarta on the library PC — what a joke.

It took thirty minutes just to load, by which point our lunch break was already gone.

And now kids today have the whole power of Google, instant knowledge at their fingertips.

They could learn about literally anything in seconds. But instead, most of them are glued to YouTube, Snapchat, TikTok, and whatever else.

If I'd had that kind of tech, my homework would've been done in half the time... and I'd have had way more gaming hours logged.

Rant 24 — Moaners and Comment Sections

Does anyone ever get sick of listening to moaning people?

Lately at work, there's been a select few who just moan, moan, moan about anything and everything, the job, the hours, the weather, the snacks in the vending machine.

And all the while, they contribute very little in the way of actual work.

Meanwhile, the poor sods who keep their heads down and graft end up picking up the slack. It's like a natural law of the workplace: the more you moan, the less you do, and the more someone else ends up doing for you.

I'm drained by it. Absolutely drained. I feel like the next moan I hear will be answered by me finally snapping:
"Oh, just shuuuuut the fuuuuuuk up, you miserable old cunt, and do some fucking work."

But even then, I already know what would happen.
The shocked pause.
The fake "Wooooow, what's wrong with him?"

And then the whispers behind my back: "What a miserable prick he is."

Me and a co-worker were talking about this one woman in particular who was like the ringleader of negativity and would go around everybody putting negative slants on things and you know what it's like at work negativity spreads like cancer,

I mean if you had never met the women and you just saw her from a short distance you would think to your self-dam she looks like a right miserable old trout, we discussed her husband and how he must of felt at home, he mentioned imagine shagging her, I was like dam face like a bulldog and she'd have tits like two bags of puke! Conversation ended there as we creased laughing.

I scroll through the net sometimes on my phone, see an article or product that catches my eye, and think: "I'll check the comments, see what people are saying."

Bad idea.

Every time, it’s the same thing — a swarm of people tearing into it. “Shit company.” “Worst product ever.” “Total scam.”
And the mad part is, 90% of them have never even touched the thing. No hands-on experience. No real knowledge of the subject. Just pure, armchair bile.

Rant 25 — Dad Dancing in the Car

I was driving my two daughters to Home Bargains so they could spend their pocket money, a common event in our house. The radio was blasting when the *Ghostbusters* theme came on. "What a fuckin' banger," I thought.

So, I did what any dad does. Rolled the windows down, cranked the volume even higher, and started driving slowly past people on the street. Bopping my head, singing along, full performance mode — the works.

And the best part? Watching my daughters shrink into themselves in the passenger seats, faces locked in that "don't look, don't react" mode. No laughs. No smiles. No joining in. Just pure survival instinct: pretend this isn't happening. I know my daughters love me, but I can't quite pinpoint the exact moment I became uncool.

I remember the days when they would scream with laughter, egging me on, encouraging me to carry on to no end.

Now? Nothing. Just stone-faced embarrassment. I suppose it's all part of being a dad. A process. One I can guarantee happens to every dad at some point — that shift from hero to cringe. And the truth is… I wouldn’t change it for the world.

Rant 26 – People Driving Vans

I'm absolutely sick of dickheads in vans, especially white ones.
There pure bellends, I'm going to assume it's little men, probably working in building sites or similar types of work, thinking they rock hard.

Probably the same types that have 3 pints down the town and then think they're 10 men and start fights. Get a fucking grip.

In my mind, these types of men have small willies and often get laughed at by women they've showed their dick pics to, the kind of laugh that carries on in the toilets long after they've left the room.

So yeh, that's my generalisation of these types of small-willied men that drive vans like knob heads.
I never see women driving in vans like this and despite the terrible driving of some of these van drivers, I've never seen one being chased by the cops or being pulled over. They're just left to continue driving like absolute tits.

Police probably let it slide because they can't be arsed with the 10-men attitude they'd get back in return. Or perhaps some of the police officers have shrivelled willies and are too timid to fight on with them.

Rant 27 — The Maggot Infested Wheely Bin

So, I went outside to put some rubbish in the wheely bin and what do you know — fucking dirty maggots are literally pouring from the side.

It was a warm summer's day, so I don't know if that gets them excited or something, but the tramps were all over the place.

They're dirty little bastards and I don't like touching them or having them around me. They make me feel dirty.

So, I did what every man would have done I got the wife to blast them with a bottle of bleach water. Took a few goes, but we finally defeated them, and they all died.

What was left was a mushy mess of dead maggots all over the rubbish, inside the lid, down the side of the bin, and on the floor around their area.

I imagined they would just dissolve away fully now or be washed away by the rain... I was wrong.

A few days later, on a warm night, it was raining and I realised I had left my phone in the car. So I went to the front door, opened it, and stepped out a few steps towards my car.

I didn't put my shoes on, and my feet got slightly wet. When I opened the car door it illuminated the driveway, and I could see little white dots. Couldn't make out exactly what it was, wasn't sure if it was something or nothing.

Anyways, I stepped back into the house and turned the outside light on — and I couldn't fuckin' believe it.

Never have I seen anything like it before. Maggots were scattered and spread out everywhere — at least in a 10-metre radius of the front door. I shouted the wife to show her.

She wasn't impressed. I wondered, how could this be? There's a concrete driveway.

Where have they all come from? Had they been rained down from the sky? Because the radius and the way they were scattered about was as if hail had landed on the floor… but instead, maggots.

I blame the local council for this. Changing when we get our wheely bins emptied. Gone from once a week to once every two weeks for general waste. Not only has it caused rat problems, but it's also caused fucking maggots taking over driveways.

Pompous MPs and council bigwigs living rich off the working classes' tax money. Council tax — £225 a month for "local services" like getting your bins emptied. Anyone with a family of four has a full overflowing bin because the wheely bin isn't big enough to hold two weeks' worth of rubbish.

But these MPs and rich council employees are living the dream. Probably only eat at home once a week because they can afford to eat out every day, so they don't have much rubbish at home. Must be nice.

Just like the UK government living rich off the working person's tax money while the rest of us can barely afford to keep a roof over our head. Fucking sick of it.

Rant 28 — The Smoke Shelter Wank Count

So, at work again, I was on my break time having a vape. Very important I get my nicotine intake. I love the conversations that go on in the smoking shelter — it's some of my best moments of the day.

On this occasion the smoke shelter was overwhelmed, as we all sat under its cover while it pissed down with rain outside. Typical English weather.

One young lad sat in the corner, and I could see his right arm shuffling. I said, *"What the fuck are you doing over there, mate?"*

He replied, *"I'm working out my forearm with this hand gripper."*
I was like, *"Ohh…"* Then another lad piped up and said, *"Yeah, he's strengthening his grip for the angry wanks he has at home." Hahahaha, I laughed*

Lad one replied, *"Yeah, I have one every two hours."*
Lad two fired back, *"Is that all? I have one about every twenty minutes."*
Lad one replied, *"Fucking hell."*

I chimed in at this point and said, *"Every twenty minutes? Every twenty minutes, aye — foreskin battered, looking like whale blubber."*
They cried with laughter. I also added, *"Your dick would be so battered and swollen that you'd no longer need lube — the blood would do the job."*

Everyone in the smoke shelter creased. I'd done my job: turned everyone's shit day into an okay day, just by making people laugh. It's one thing I'm good at.

We all went back into work happier, already looking forward to the next break.

Rant 29 — Tit Head and the Horsefly

In my early twenties — about 22 or 23, I can't remember exactly, I lived in the Nevada desert for about four years in a small town called Hawthorne. It was a tiny place, about one mile square in size.

Regardless of its size, it had all the everyday American-type places you'd expect: a McDonald's, a casino called the Renata, a petrol station, and just your average corner-shop-style stores surrounded by houses.

Hawthorne gave off those *Hills Have Eyes* type vibes. A lot of the people there were your general redneck type. There was a lot of drug-related activity going on, I guess that was one way for people to make money in such a small town. But I'll say no more about that.

I got in with a wild type of people about my age — easy-going, carefree types with no thought for the future, not much more than the day we were living in. Every day for about six months we spent our days together.

That summer was extremely hot, especially for me, someone used to the English climate.

We drank all day, fooled about. One of my friends had a pool table in his driveway, and sometimes we'd drink and gather around it about the same time every day, just having fun. It was great.

One day a bunch of us lads and girls or as it was often referred to their back then bros and hoes ha-ha, we drove out to a lake that wasn't too far away.

Perfect place to be in the summer when it was red hot. Beers in hand, splashing and fooling around, having a laugh. It really was great — except you did tend to get the odd horsefly there.

And in Nevada, these things are pretty fucking big, take more than a rolled-up newspaper to sort one of these little twats out.

I'd say about the size of a cockroach, but flying around like your average housefly.

Anyway, the reason I've been mentioning all the above is because I have this one memory of us being in the lake, and it's about a moment when one of my mates was still in the water alone while the rest of us chilled on the shore. A hilarious memory.

He was bouncing about in the water, shouting for us all to come back in.

As we gazed at him, we noticed a blackish blob right on his forehead, dead centre. Easy to see, since his head was already balding — something we often teased him about. Somehow, he hadn't noticed it.

We waved at him and shouted, *"You have a fucking horsefly on your head!"* He put his hands around his head trying to knock it off but, as usual in this kind of comical situation, he completely missed it.

We continued shouting, *"It's still on your head, you fucking gimp!"* Looking panicked, he just thought *fuck it* and went under water for a few seconds.
He came back up and it was gone. We shouted, *"Yeah, you're okay!"* But literally as we finished speaking — smack — it landed back in the exact same spot.

We howled with laughter, screaming at him, *"It's back! It's still there!"* He was convinced we were bullshitting, waving his hands over his head looking for it again, missing it entirely. We continued shouting while also laughing our tits off.

He went under again and came back up, and again it was gone.

We laughed amongst ourselves about the thought of it coming back a third time. Meanwhile my mate in the lake, a slightly tubby guy, started powerwalking as fast as he could back to shore, making waves and splashing everywhere.

Then it happened. It landed again. Third time, same spot. We could barely scream to him that it was back, because by then we were dying for breath with laughter.

How he couldn't feel it, I'll never understand. But he definitely felt what happened next. He screamed in pain. It bit him.

Horseflies bite hard — especially ones that big. We very nearly died now with laughter — I mean really died.

He made it back to shore, but the fly was still at him, zipping past him here and there. He was almost crying in pain, an instant lump rising from the bite. It looked like a fucking nipple.

I named him Tit Head. Then so did everyone else. For the rest of that summer, that was his name. This memory often makes me laugh. Feels unreal that it was almost twenty years ago now. Feels like last month.

I lost touch with all of them within two years of that event. I feel sad about that, and I often wonder what they're up to now in that small town so far away — so small it basically doesn't exist.

Rant 30 — The Arse Whisperer

I've mentioned before that I have a Labrador, but I also have a Staffy. He's about fourteen years old now, getting on a bit, but still has a lot of energy.

This one loves me. He follows me everywhere. He goes to bed when I go to bed, he wakes up when I wake up. He lays next to me on the couch, in the bed, and sometimes he even sits next to me while I'm trying to take a shit on the toilet.

Anyway, this dog loves me, and I love him. He's literally my best friend, if I'm being honest, and I'd be lost without him.

Somehow, some way, I've managed to train this dog to leap to attention — even from a deep sleep on the couch — at the speed of light. He'll spin in circles or launch straight at my Labrador.

This is where it gets funny — even strange. I've managed to deliver this command in the form of a fart. The better the rip, the more hyper he goes.

There can be dead silence in the living room, and I can destroy that silence with a juicy wet one — and then comes the aftermath.

Jax, my Staffy, goes ballistic: messing up rugs, spinning, making a massive racket with his paws slapping on the laminate floor.

The look on my terrified Lab's face when it happens is pure fear, bracing herself for the unpredictable chaos that might come next. It's like a war chant to Jax — rip a fart and he's battle-ready. Never seen anything like it.

I will try to catch it on video, and I'll post it on social media. Anyone interested can find my social media details at the end of the book. I guarantee either disgust or laughter.

31. Piss Poor Poem

Here is a little something to summarise
everything we've experienced here.

I'm forty-two years old and life's on pause,
Staring at my gut and its pregnant deform.

Work shifts grind me, alarms make me twitch,
But fuck it, PS5, I ain't rich, I'm a glitch.

My brain's an onion, peeling in space,
Aliens plotting while I lie in place.

And yet when I'm up, in Sainsbury's queue,
"Cheers, mate" slipped out wrong pronoun, oops,
poo!

My belly balloons though my diet's the same,
Laxatives, toilets, my arse takes the blame.

Voices keep shouting, "Give up!" / "Try hard!"
I tell the whole lot: "Fuck off, you retards."
The wife brought a hedgehog house, twenty-five
quid,

Not one bastard hedgehog has ever moved in.

Work's smoke shelter's buzzing, wasps dive like

jets,
And I'm sat there vaping, observing the wasp deaths.

"Two Girls One Cup" scarred me deep in the brain,
Now prostate exams feel like bum-rape in vain.
Never had wet dreams, sheets always dry,
Granny bum-shuffles, fart-steps by.

Queefs in sex, the awkward blast,
Do you laugh, ignore, or just shag fast?

Dreams of A.I. and robots ahead,
While I'm charging myself on the couch thinking "am I fucked in the head"?

Weird little urges to slap or to kick,
Don't act on them, but they're still there, thick.

Women don't fart, at least in my head,
Till the wife takes a dump and the bathroom smells dead.
Moaners at work, two bags of puke tits,
Council, MPs, all full of shit.

Dad dancing to Ghostbusters, kids want to hide,
Embarrassed as fuck while I beam with pride.

Tit-Head in Nevada with horsefly bite,
Nipple on his forehead, what a fucking sight.

And last but not least, the Arse Whisperer tale,
My fart is a trumpet, my Staffy chases his tail.

He spins like a maniac, Lab hides in dread,
One fart from my arse and the house goes red.

So that's Volume One — my life on display,
Shits, farts, odd thoughts, and work's foul play.

If you've laughed, then my job's been done,
This ain't Shakespeare — it's *The Man Rants* Volume One.

Afterword

Thank you for taking the time to read this book. Everything you've just read came straight from my head and my heart. Some parts may have been raw, blunt, or even offensive — but that was never my intention. I just wanted to be honest, and to put my thoughts down the way they really are.

I'd really love to hear what you think — whether you can relate, completely disagree, or just want to share your own thoughts.

You can follow me and reach out at @shizymcnizy on x (twitter) or follow me on TikTok @imakebook2025 or email me directly at imakebooks2025@gmail.com.

And just to clarify I mean no offence to anyone I'm just saying what pops in my head before thought kicks in most the time......I don't want any of you soft fannies to get offended

Thanks again for giving me your time.

— *Matthew R. Mcmillan*

www.ingramcontent.com/pod-product-compliance
Ingram Content Group UK Ltd.
Pitfield, Milton Keynes, MK11 3LW, UK
UKHW021500181125
9040UKWH00027B/200

9 798265 225771